GUITAR WITH TABLATURE

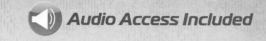 Audio Access Included

Wedding Songs for CLASSICAL GUITAR

Guitar performed by Doug Boduch

T0081326

To access companion recorded performances online, visit:
www.halleonard.com/mylibrary

Enter Code
6758-2531-9967-1470

ISBN 978-1-4950-0253-3

HAL•LEONARD®
CORPORATION
7777 W. BLUEMOUND RD. P.O. BOX 13819 MILWAUKEE, WI 53213

In Australia Contact:
Hal Leonard Australia Pty. Ltd.
4 Lentara Court
Cheltenham, Victoria, 3192 Australia
Email: ausadmin@halleonard.com.au

Visit Hal Leonard Online at
www.halleonard.com

CONTENTS

Air
from WATER MUSIC

By George Frideric Handel

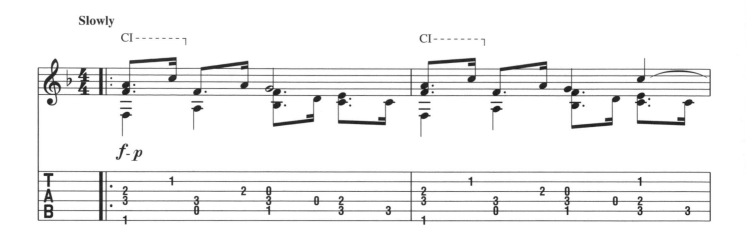

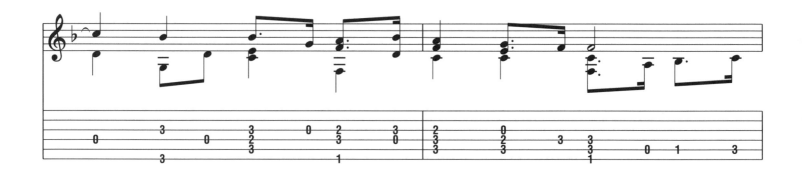

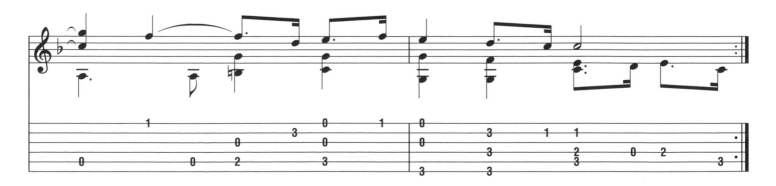

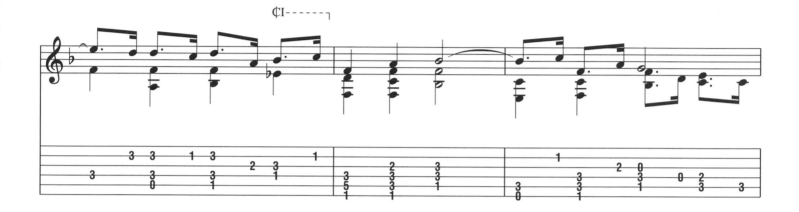

Air on the G String

from ORCHESTRAL SUITE NO. 3

By Johann Sebastian Bach

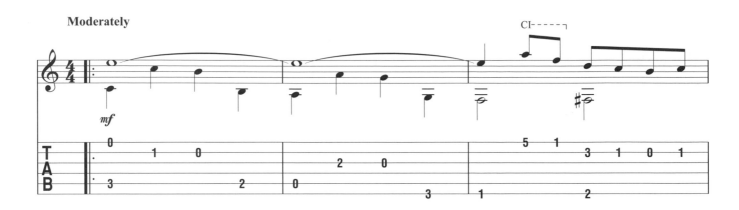

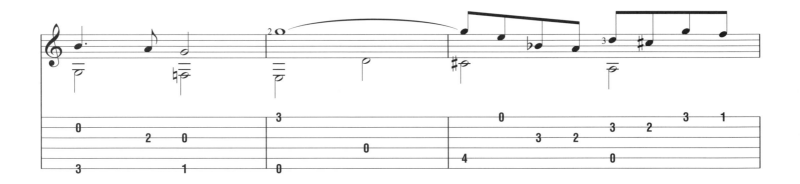

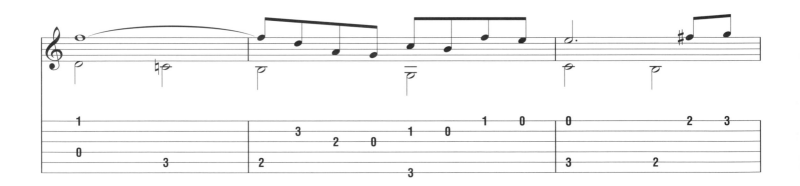

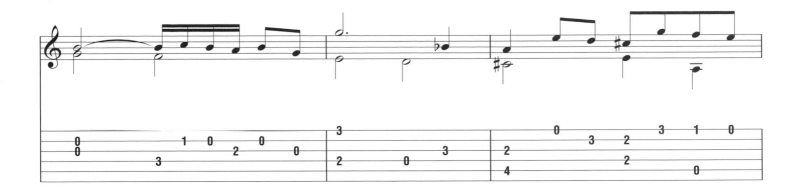

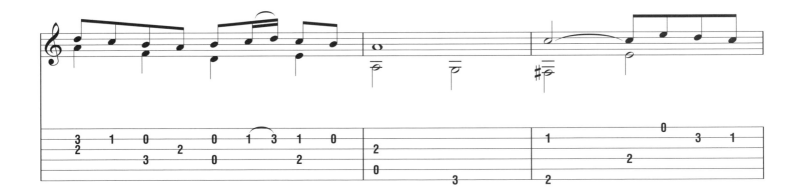

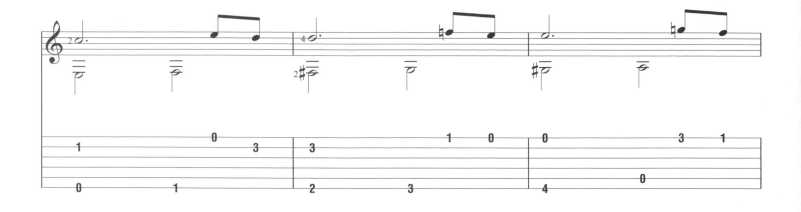

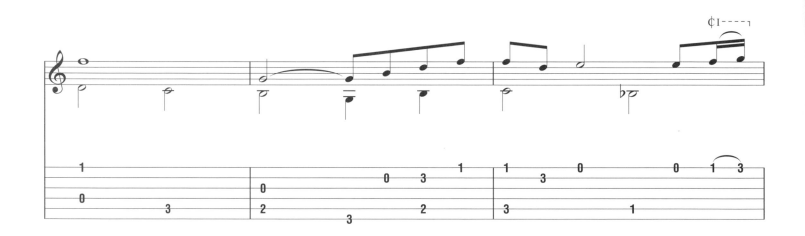

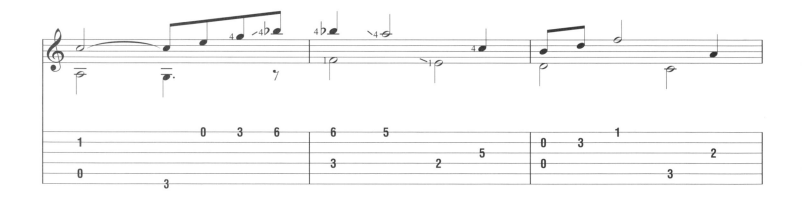

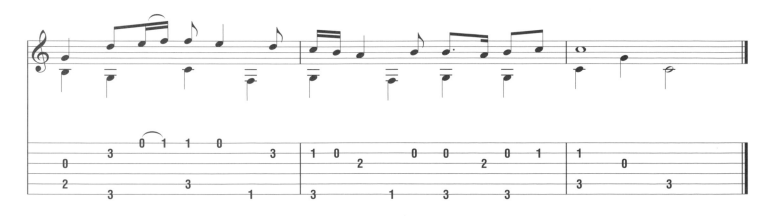

Allegro Maestoso

from WATER MUSIC

By George Frideric Handel

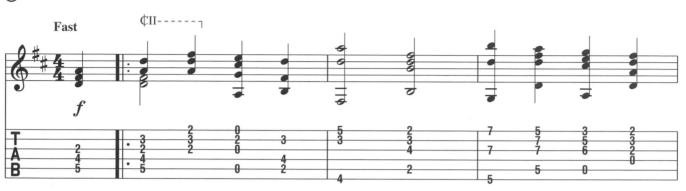

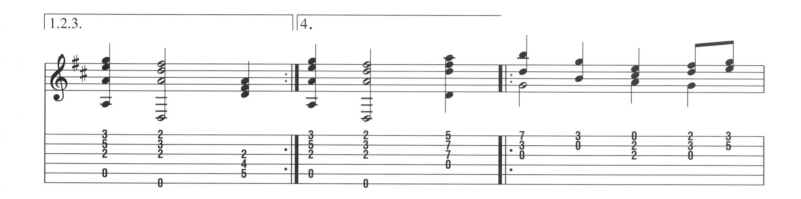

Ave Maria

By Franz Schubert

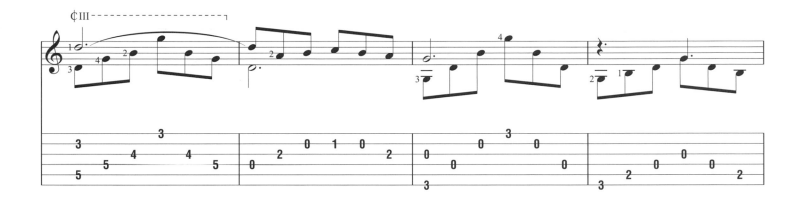

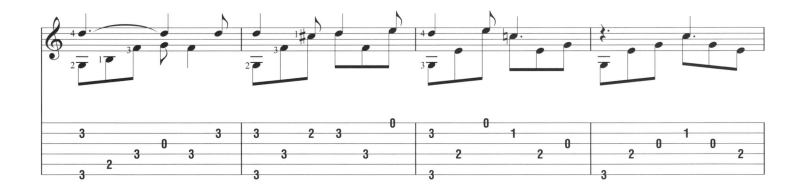

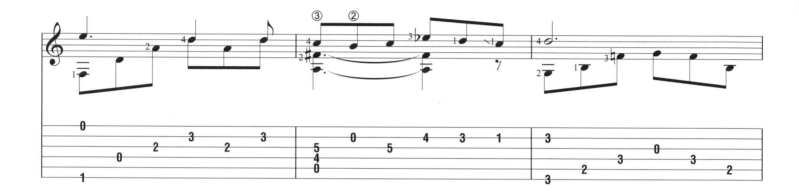

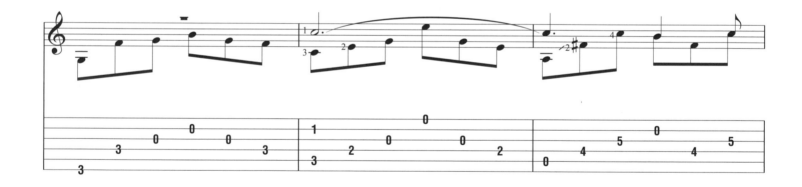

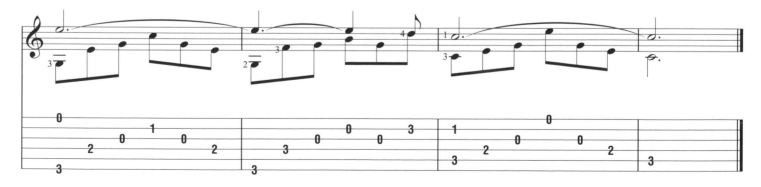

Barcarolle

from THE TALES OF HOFFMANN (LES CONTES D'HOFFMANN)

By Jacques Offenbach

⑥ = D

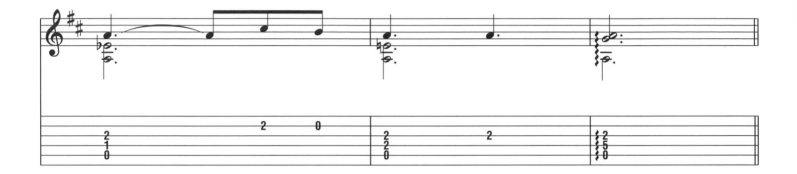

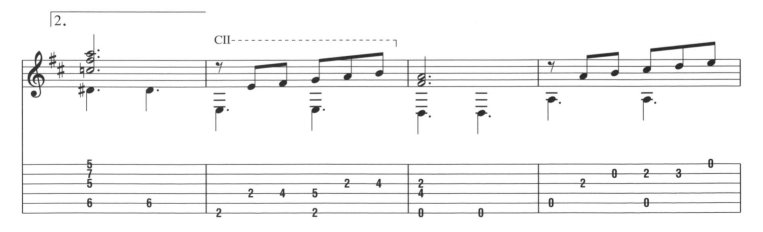

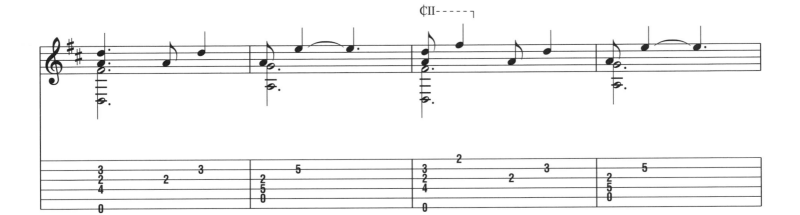

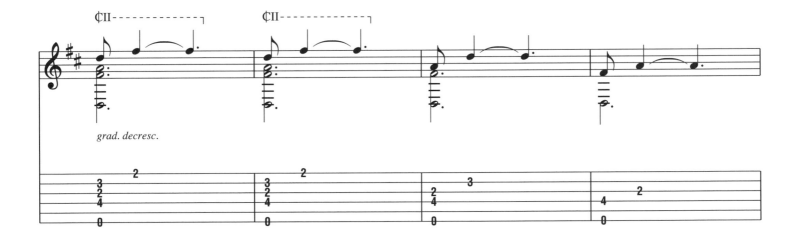

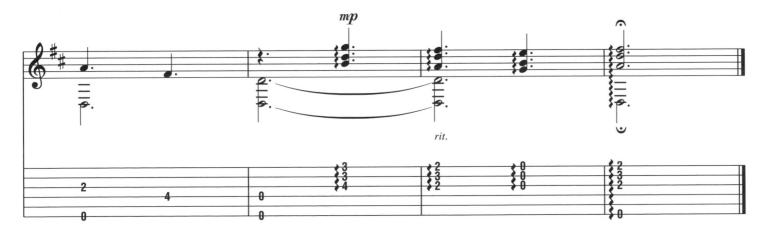

Ave Verum
(Jesu, Word of God Incarnate)

By Wolfgang Amadeus Mozart

Slowly, in 2

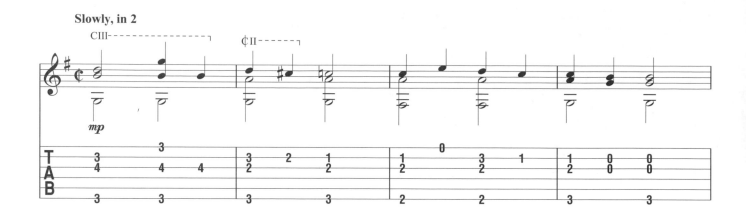

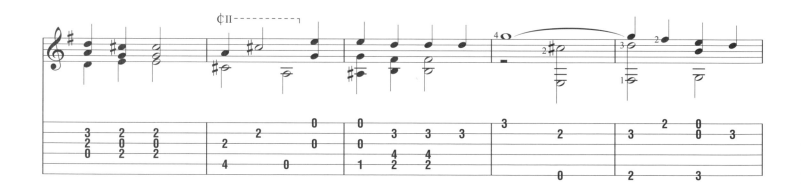

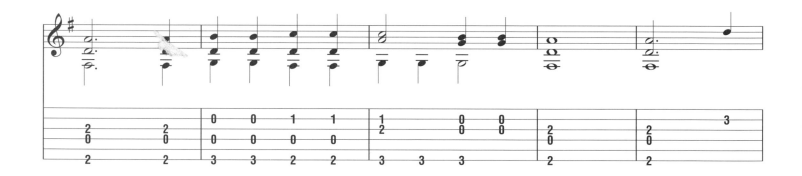

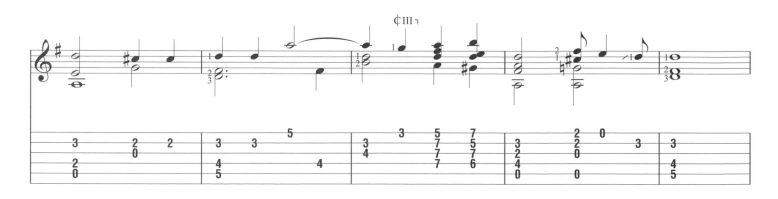

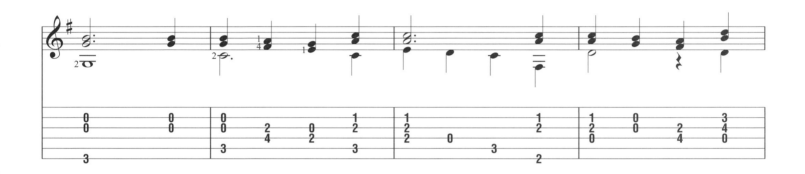

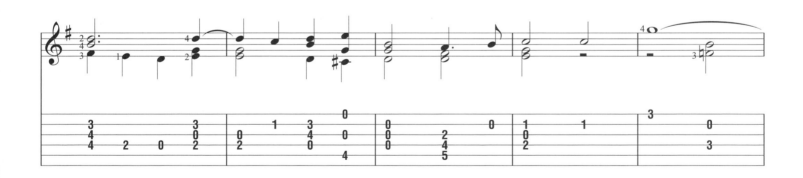

Bridal Chorus
from LOHENGRIN

By Richard Wagner

Drop D tuning:
(low to high) D-A-D-G-B-E

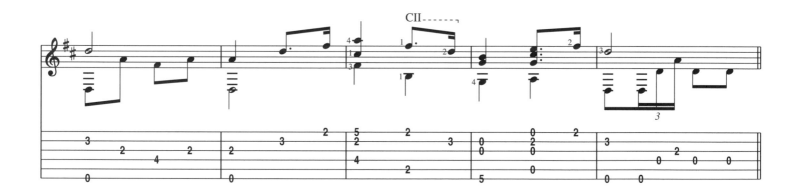

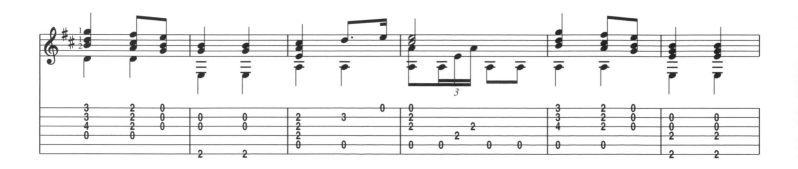

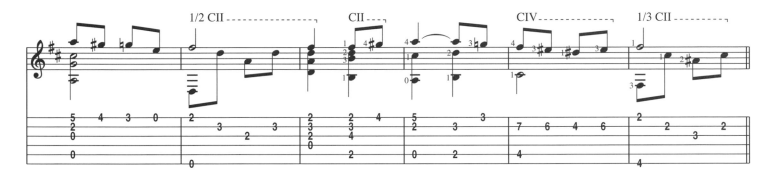

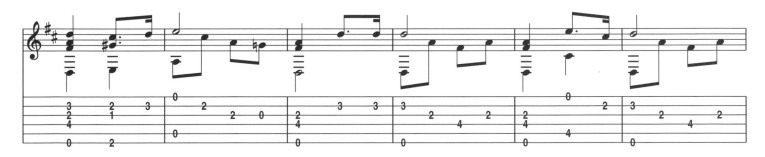

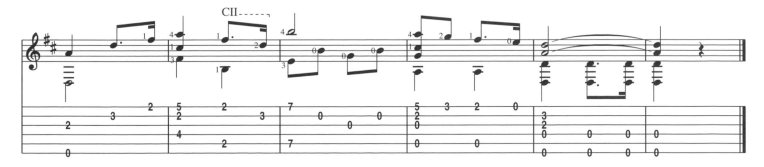

Canon in D

By Johann Pachelbel

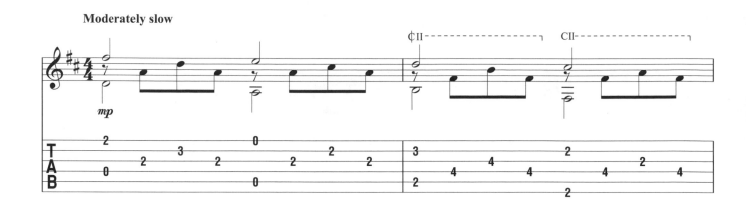

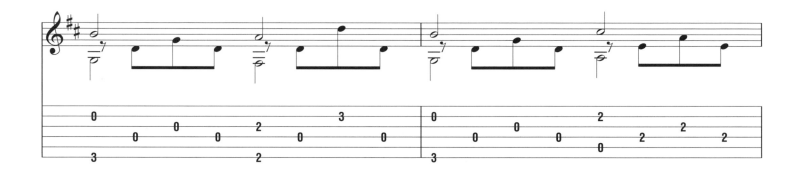

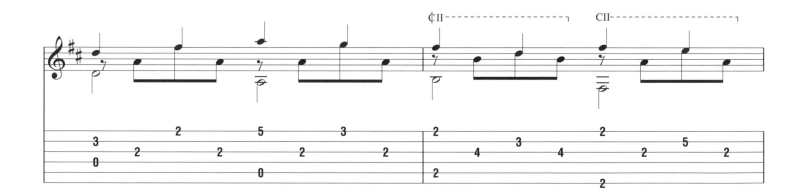

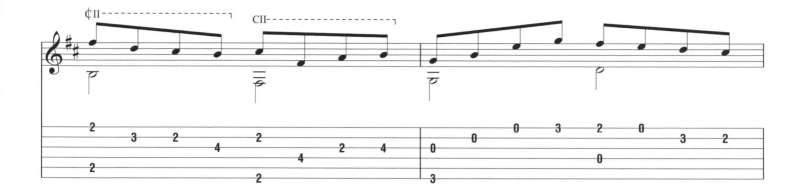

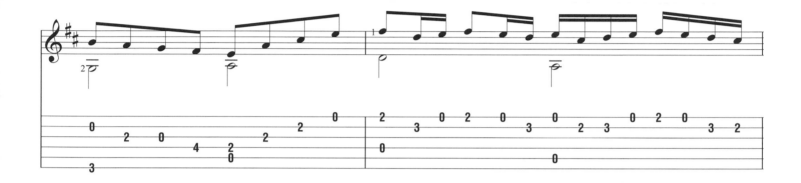

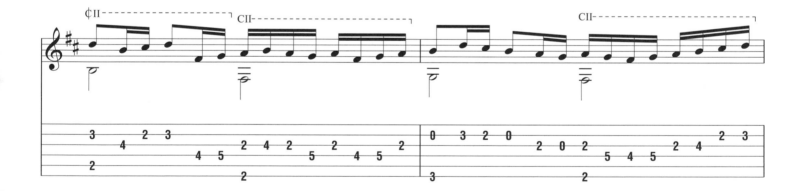

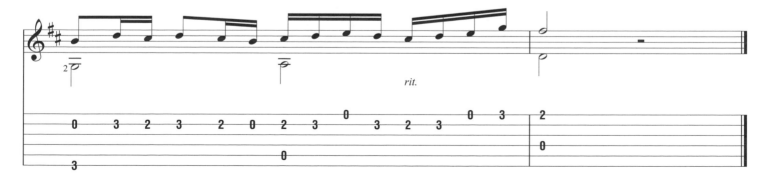

Caro Mio Ben

Text from an Anonymous Italian poem
Music by Tommaso Giordani

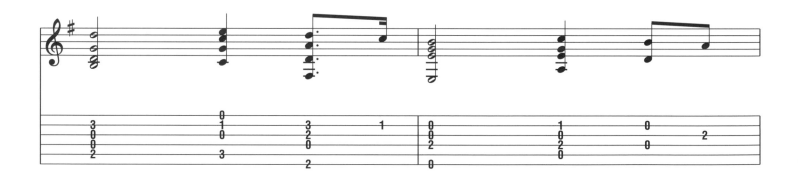

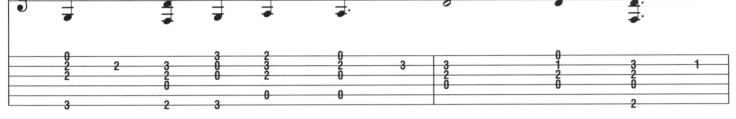

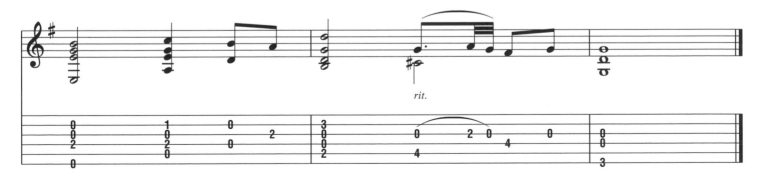

Dance of the Spirits

from ORFEO ED EURIDICE

By Christoph Willibald von Gluck

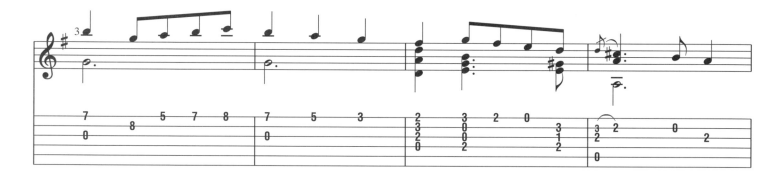

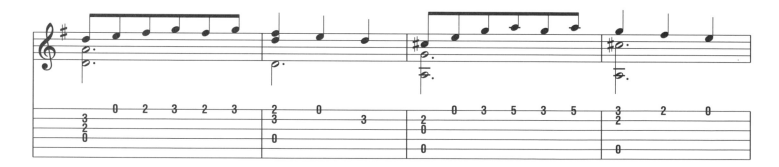

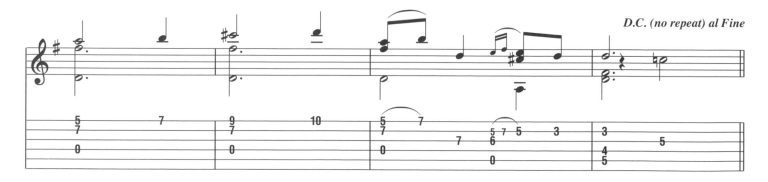

Hornpipe

from WATER MUSIC

By George Frideric Handel

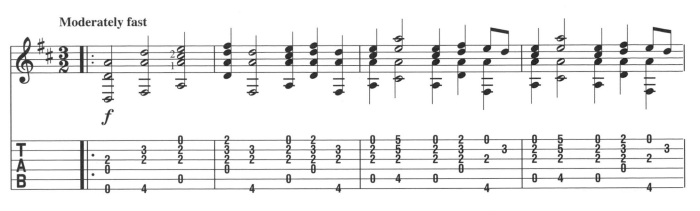

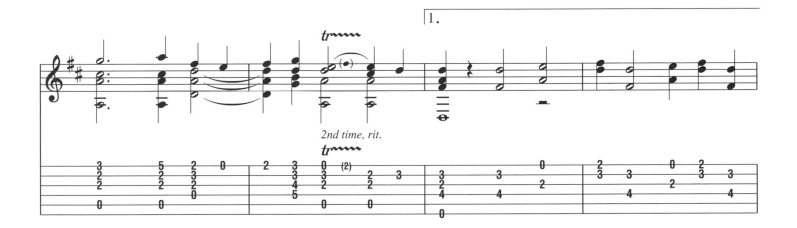

Intermezzo
from CAVALLERIA RUSTICANA

By Pietro Mascagni

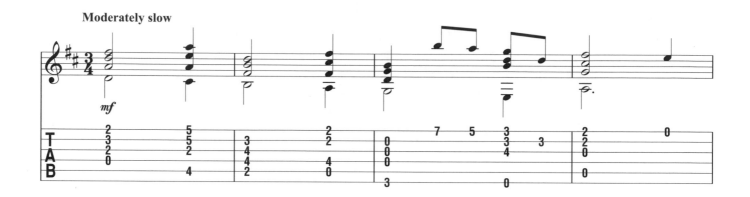

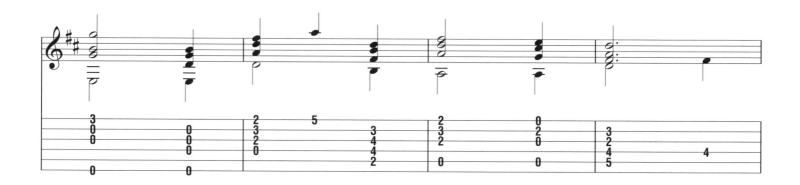

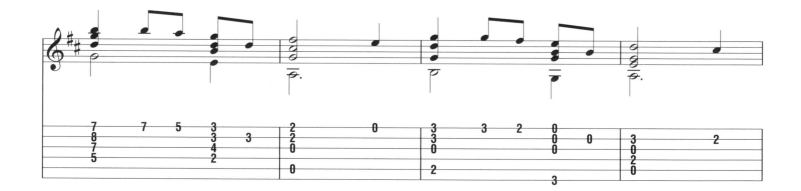

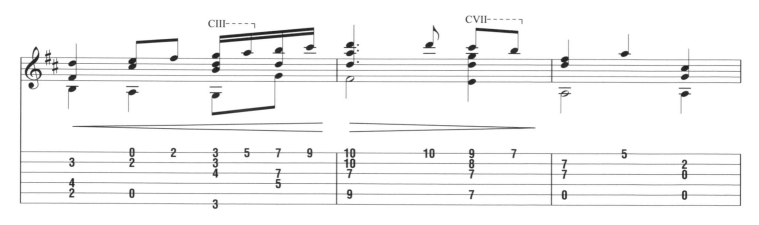

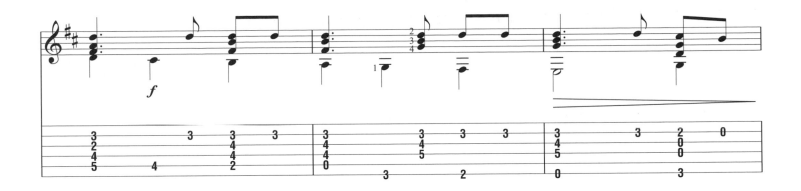

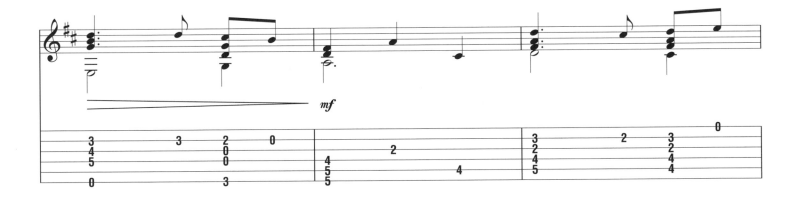

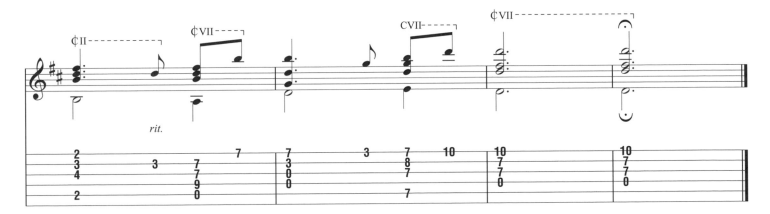

Jesu, Joy of Man's Desiring

English Words by Robert Bridges
Music by Johann Sebastian Bach

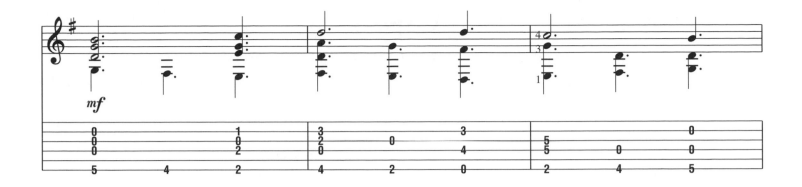

Largo

from THE FOUR SEASONS - WINTER: SECOND MOVEMENT

By Antonio Vivaldi

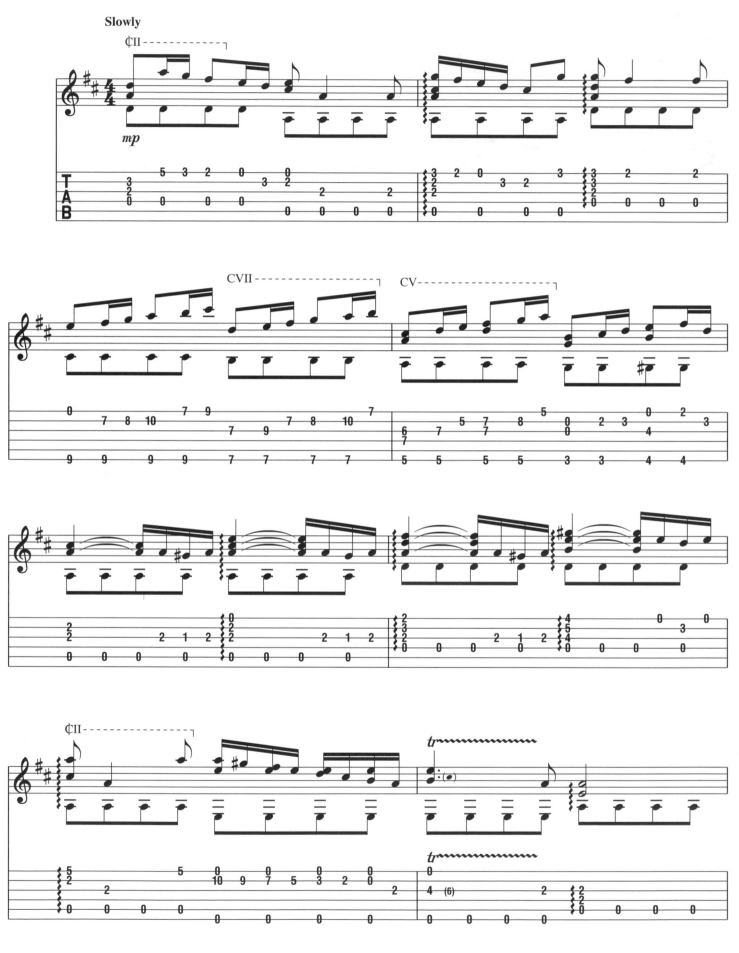

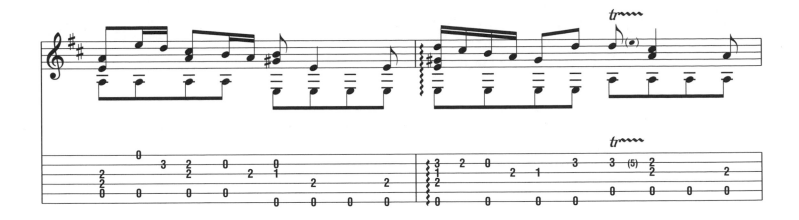

Minuet
from THE STRING QUARTET IN E MAJOR, OP. 11, NO. 5

By Luigi Boccherini

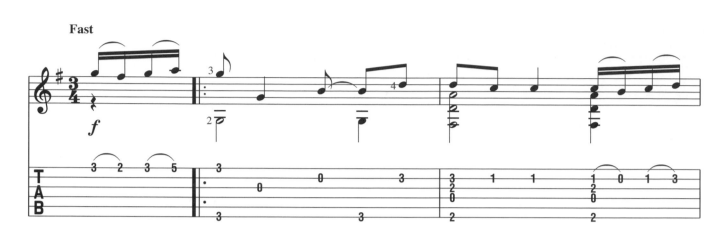

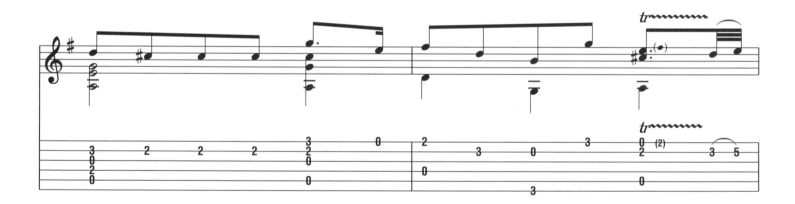

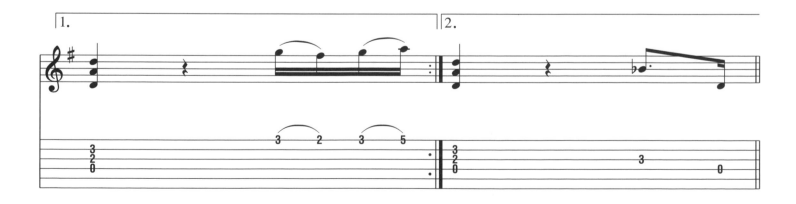

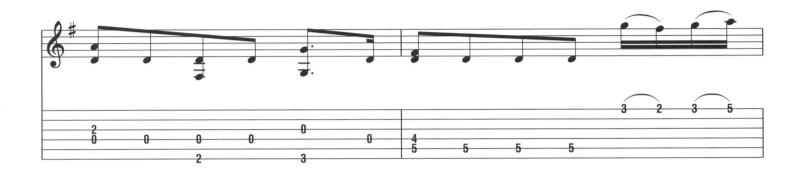

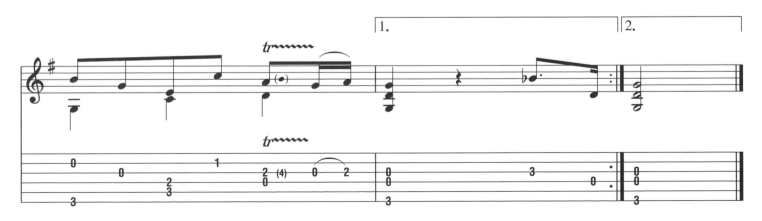

Minuet in G

from the ANNA MAGDALENA NOTEBOOK (originally for keyboard)

By Johann Sebastian Bach

Moderately

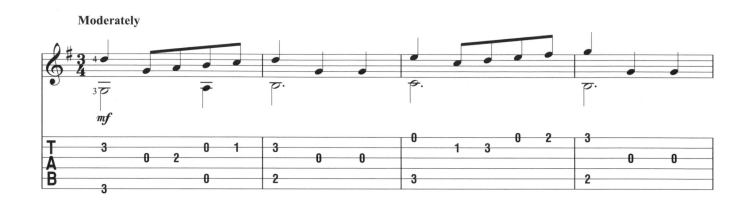

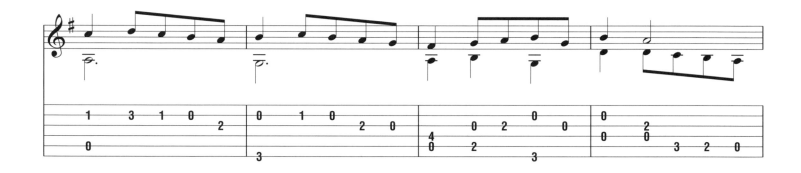

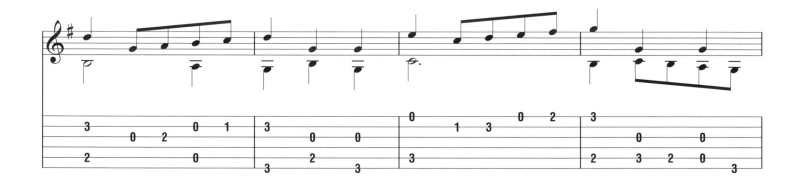

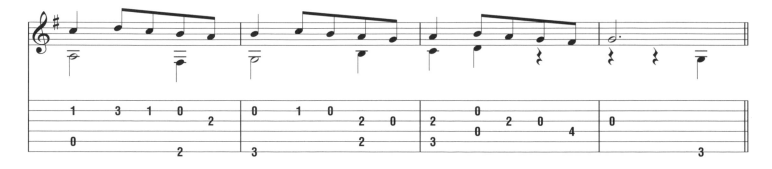

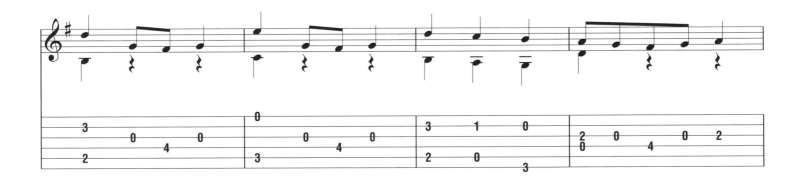

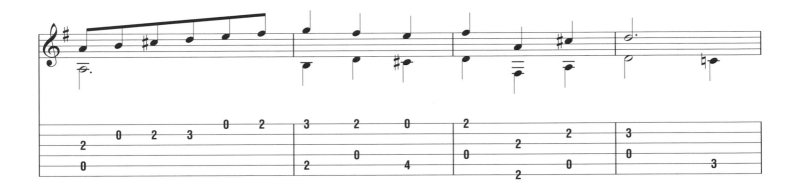

Ode to Joy

from SYMPHONY NO. 9 IN D MINOR, FOURTH MOVEMENT CHORAL THEME

Words by Henry van Dyke
Music by Ludwig van Beethoven

Prince of Denmark's March

By Jeremiah Clarke

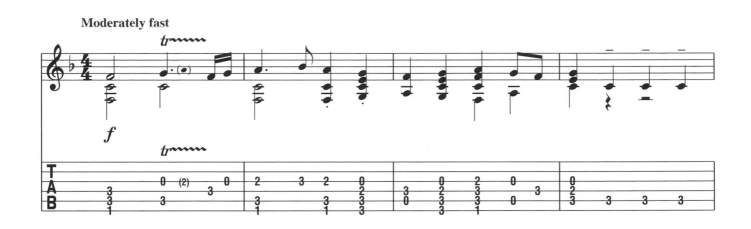

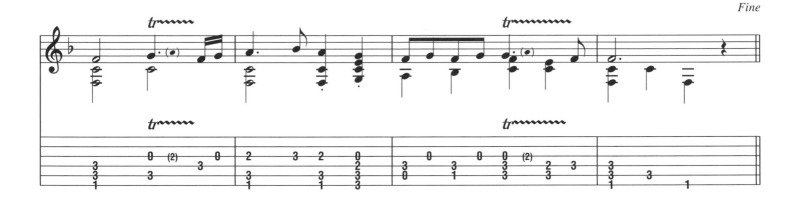

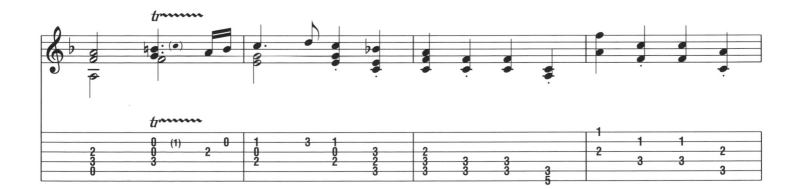

Panis Angelicus
(O Lord Most Holy)

By Cesar Franck

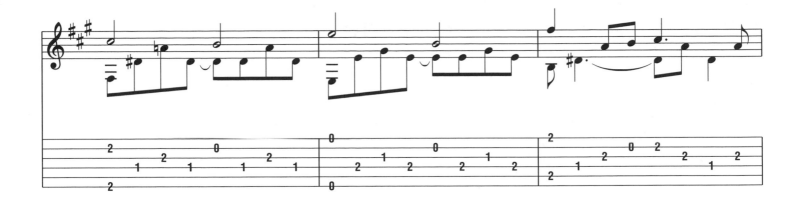

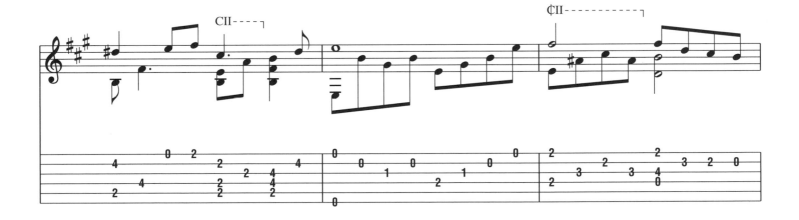

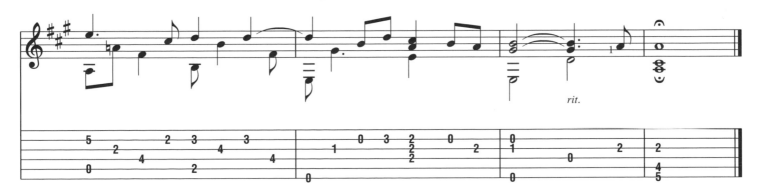

Pavane

By Gabriel Fauré

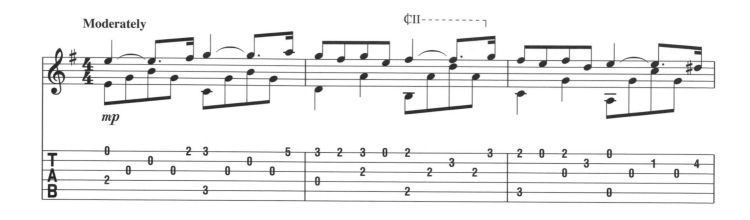

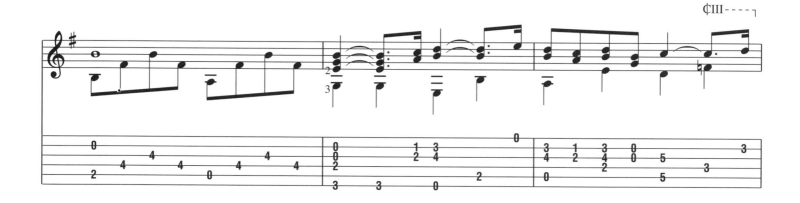

To Coda ⊕

₵II

₵II

D.C. al Coda

⊕ **Coda**

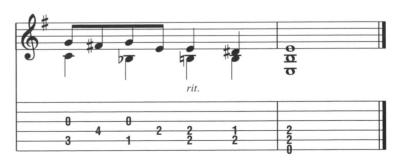

rit.

Rondeau

By Jean-Joseph Mouret

Spring, First Movement

from THE FOUR SEASONS

By Antonio Vivaldi

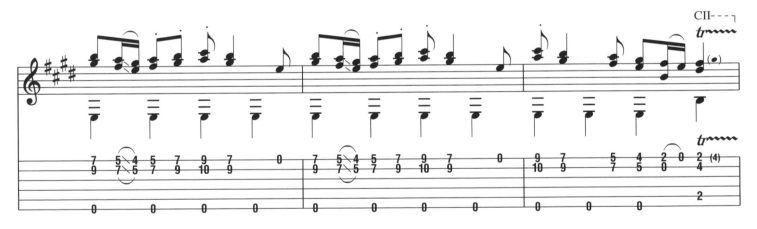

Sheep May Safely Graze

from CANTATA NO. 208

By Johann Sebastian Bach

Slowly, in 2

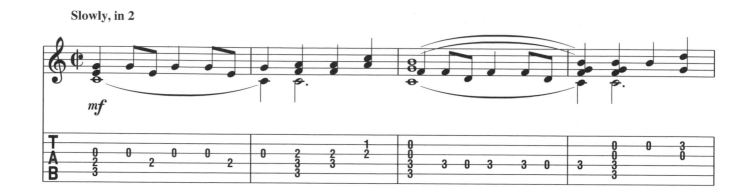

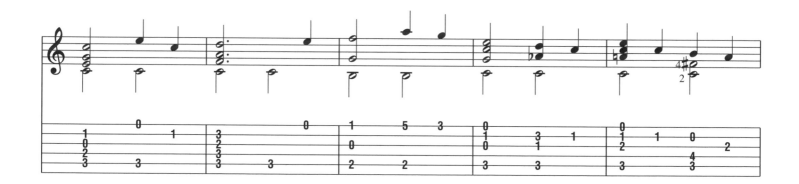

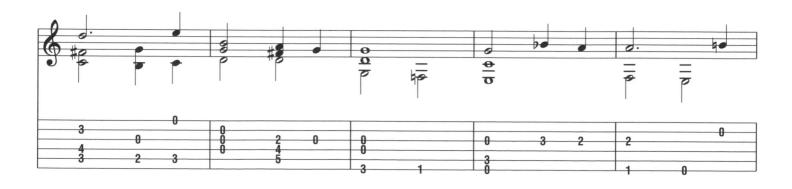

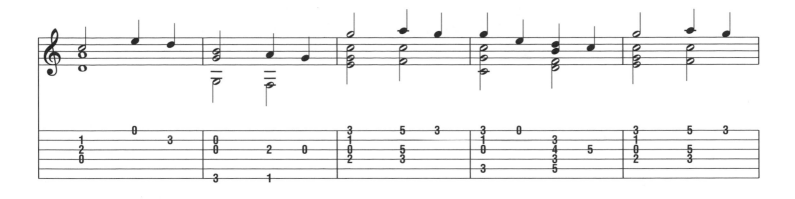

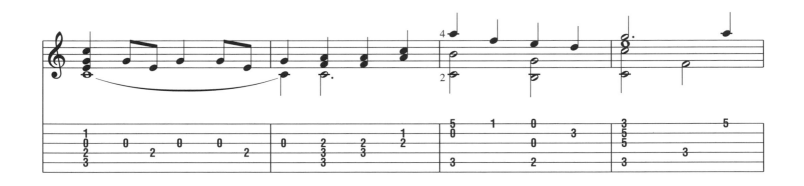

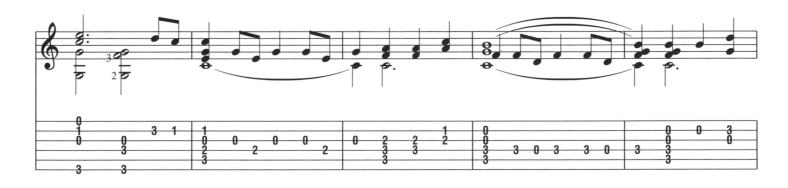

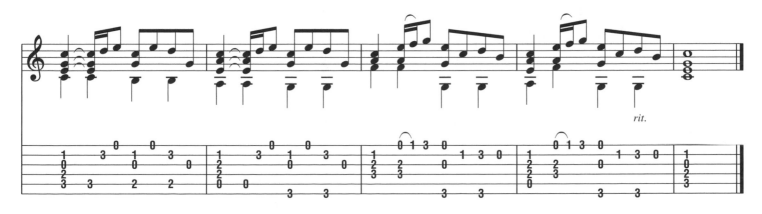

Wedding March

from A MIDSUMMER NIGHT'S DREAM

By Felix Mendelssohn

Moderately fast

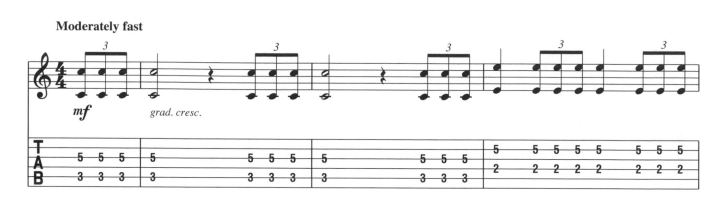

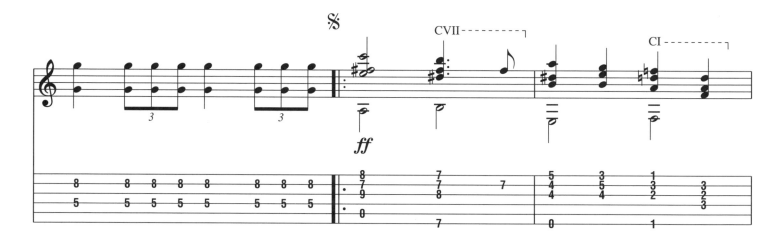

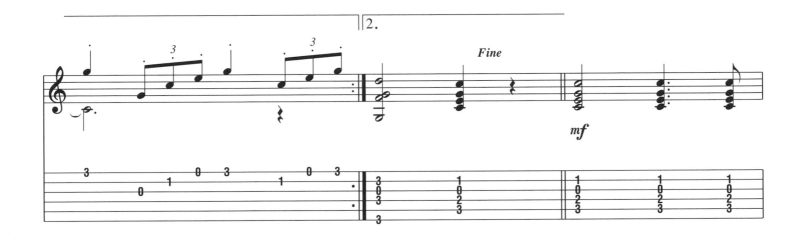

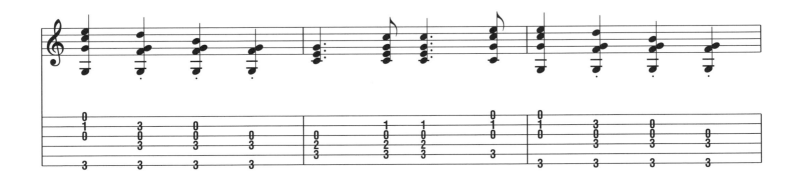

Trumpet Tune

By Jeremiah Clarke

Moderately fast

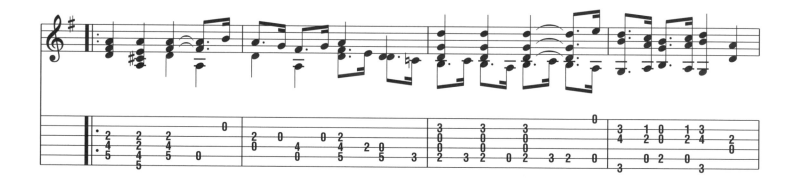